The Wonder of

Books edited by Phyllis Hobe
Published by The Westminster Press

The Wonder of Prayer
The Wonder of Love
The Wonder of Comfort

The Wonder of Prayer

**Edited by
Phyllis Hobe**

*Drawings by
Jennifer Cole*

**Bridgebooks
Philadelphia**

Book Design by Alice Derr

First edition

Bridgebooks
Published by The Westminster Press®
Philadelphia, Pennsylvania

PRINTED IN THE UNITED STATES OF AMERICA
9 8 7 6 5 4 3 2 1

Library of Congress Cataloging in Publication Data

Main entry under title:

The Wonder of prayer.

   Includes indexes.
   1. Prayer—Quotations, maxims, etc. I. Hobe,
Phyllis.
BV213.W6 1982   248.3′2   82-8317
ISBN 0-664-26002-0   AACR2

Contents

Acknowledgments

"I Yield Thee Praise," by Philip Jerome Cleveland, is used by permission of the author.

"A Whiff of Lilacs," "Balancing," and "Sing God's Praises," from *Because I Love You,* by Alice Joyce Davidson. Copyright © 1982 by Alice Joyce Davidson. Published by Fleming H. Revell Company. Used by permission.

"A Busy Mother's Prayer" © 1959, 1967 by Marjorie Holmes Mighell. From the book *Love and Laughter,* by Marjorie Holmes. Reprinted by permission of Doubleday & Company, Inc. "New Day" from *Hold Me Up a Little Longer, Lord,* by Marjorie Holmes. Copyright © 1971, 1972, 1973, 1974, 1975, 1976, 1977 by Marjorie Holmes Mighell. Reprinted by permission of Doubleday & Company, Inc.

"Today, Lord, our son/daughter goes to school," by Tony Jasper, from *The Illustrated Family Prayer Book,* edited by Tony Jasper. Copyright © 1981 by Tony Jasper/London Editions. Used by permission of The Seabury Press, Inc.

"They came for our child, Lord," by Tony Jasper, from *The Illustrated Family Prayer Book,* edited by Tony Jasper. Copyright © 1981 by Tony Jasper/London Editions. Used by permission of The Seabury Press, Inc.

"Today, Lord, has been awful!" by Flora Larsson, S.A., from *The Illustrated Family Prayer Book,* edited by Tony Jasper. Copyright © 1981 by Tony Jasper/London Editions. Used by permission of The Seabury Press, Inc.

Introduction

by Colleen Townsend Evans

Communication is the lifeline of any relationship . . . and no relationship can develop beyond the level of its communication. So it is that prayer is vital to our relationship with God, because it is through prayer that we communicate with God.

Sometimes we may not even use words when we pray, but may simply experience an outpouring of our deepest feelings. At other times we are aware only of God, and as our spirits listen, we are impregnated with his message for our lives. As Edwin Keith describes it, "Prayer is exhaling the spirit of man and inhaling the spirit of God." And, always, communication must go in both directions.

Praying does not interrupt life. It is part of life, and there are many ways and times to pray. Even as we do our work and interact with others, we can turn to God at any moment for help, for guidance, for strength. The key to prayer is the attitude of our hearts, for God hears beyond our words to what we truly feel and mean. Communicating with God is natural and real to all of us. There is no area of our lives or our world it cannot express.

It is my prayer that the selections in this book will encourage you, as they have me, to "rise up and draw near to God in mind, and in heart, and in spirit" (Alexander Whyte).

I. Life Enrichment

"... To make this life worth-while ..."
George Eliot

Ten minutes spent in Christ's society every day, ay, two minutes, if it be face to face, and heart to heart, will make the whole life different.

William Drummond

We meet God in Spirit and through Him, we meet each other. And the Spirit is much greater than life itself and bigger than feeble, little words that a human mind could express.

Helen Steiner Rice

It is only when men begin to worship that they begin to grow.

Calvin Coolidge

Come, Lord, work upon us. Set us on fire and clasp us close, be fragrant to us, draw us to Thy loveliness: let us love, let us run to Thee.

St. Augustine

THE SECRET

I met God in the morning,
When my day was at its best,
And His presence came like sunrise
With a glory in my breast.

All day long the Presence lingered,
All day long He stayed with me;
And we sailed in perfect calmness
O'er a very troubled sea.

Other ships were blown and battered,
Other ships were sore distressed,
But the winds that seemed to drive them
Brought to us both peace and rest.

Then I thought of other mornings,
With a keen remorse of mind,
When I too had loosed the moorings,
With the Presence left behind.

So I think I know the secret,
Learned from many a troubled way—;
You must seek Him in the morning,
If you want Him through the day!

Ralph Spaulding Cushman

Tell God all that is in your heart, as one unloads one's heart to a dear friend. People who have no secrets from each other never want subjects of conversation; they do not weigh their words, because there is nothing to be kept back. Neither do they seek for something to say; they talk out of the abundance of their hearts, just what they think. Blessed are they who attain to such familiar, unreserved intercourse with God.

François de Fénelon

AN EASTER PRAYER

O God of Easter, God of resurrection power,
Bring heavenly life to our earthbound souls;
Thou, who did'st call Lazarus forth from his tomb,
Call us forth from dead works, and let our hearts be
    aglow with immortal glory and power.
Call us out of the tomb of hollow profession,
Of cold creeds, and wordy ritual,
And let Thy life abundant permeate and saturate our
    stagnant souls.
Bring joy where there is heaviness of heart;
Bring peace where there is confusion;
Bring love where there is bitterness;
And may we henceforth live in the glorious glow of
The Life which that first Easter poured forth upon a
    world of darkness.
And may we always be mindful of the Source of this life-
    giving power,
And come to Thee regularly to be refilled.
In the Savior's name,
Amen.

Author unknown

After this manner therefore pray ye:
Our Father which art in heaven,
Hallowed be thy name.
Thy kingdom come. Thy will be done in earth, as it is in
heaven.
Give us this day our daily bread.
And forgive us our debts, as we forgive our debtors.
And lead us not into temptation, but deliver us from
evil:
For thine is the kingdom, and the power, and the glory,
for ever. Amen.

Matthew 6:9–13

There are so many ways and so many times to pray,
because praying doesn't mean that we interrupt life. It's
part of life. In fact, prayer keeps us going in the midst of
our daily struggles, our ups and downs. Jesus knew
that—for he couldn't live without this direct, personal
contact with his Father. And neither can we.

Colleen Townsend Evans

A PRAYER

Give me a good digestion, Lord,
And also something to digest,
Give me a healthy body, Lord,
And sense enough to keep it at its best.
Give me a healthy mind, O Lord,
To keep the good and pure in sight,
Which seeing sin is not appalled
But finds a way to set it right.
Give me a mind that is not bound
That does not whimper, whine or sigh.
Don't let me worry overmuch
About this funny thing called I.
Give me a sense of humor, Lord,
And sense enough to see a joke,
To get more happiness out of life
And pass it on to other folk.

Author unknown

MAKING THIS LIFE WORTH-WHILE

May every soul that touches mine—
Be it the slightest contact—
Get therefrom some good;
Some little grace; one kindly thought;
One aspiration yet unfelt;
One bit of courage
For the darkening sky;

One gleam of faith
To brave the thickening ills of life;
One glimpse of brighter skies
Beyond the gathering mists—
To make this life worth-while . . .

George Eliot

LOOK UP AND LIVE

This business of living was meant to be more
    Than plodding along each day
With head bowed down and eyes on the ground
    While Time ticks the hours away.

God made this world a delightful place
    With beauty everywhere—
The grass, the flowers, the trees, the sky,
    The tang of clean, fresh air—

A world to be lived in, laughed in, loved,
    To be met with joy and zest,
A world with a challenge for each of us
    To give it our very best.

This business of living was never meant
    As a treadmill sort of thing;
There are rivers to cross, and mountains to climb,
    And glorious songs to sing!

Helen Lowrie Marshall

II. Guidance

"... He will bring you safely through ..."
Helen Steiner Rice

I walk with God daily.

Helen Keller

Help us this day, O God, to serve Thee devoutly, and the world busily, May we do our work wisely, give succour secretly, go to our meat appetitely, sit thereat discreetly, arise temperately, please our friend duly, go to bed merrily, sleep surely; for joy of our Lord Jesus Christ.

Medieval prayer

TWO WAYS

To every soul there openeth
A high way and a low;
The high soul climbs the high way
The low soul gropes the low,
And in between, on the misty flats,
The rest drift to and fro.

To every soul there openeth
A high way and a low;
And every man decideth
Which way his soul shall go.

John Oxenham

ADVERBS

May I seek to live this day
        quietly, easily,
leaning on Your mighty strength
        trustfully, restfully,
meeting others in the path
        peacefully, joyously,
waiting for Your will's unfolding
        patiently, serenely,
facing what tomorrow brings
        confidently, courageously.

Author unknown

Just think what it means to know that the Lord is *your* Shepherd and that He is leading you and anointing your scars and heart-hurt with the balm of His love. . . . You can heal your body and mind and heart with this psalm. God promises to restore your soul, revive your weary body, take you into a cool, clear place where you can rest and, no matter how steep the hill or mountain is, the Lord is going to climb it with you.

Just writing this has already given me strength. The sheep are never afraid, because they know the Shepherd will lead them into green pastures, beside the still waters. And so, as you come to "dark places" in your life, just reach out for the Hand of the Shepherd. If you stop and get very quiet and still, you will feel the Presence of God.

I often say this when I am troubled, and I imagine I am just a "little lamb" who doesn't know where to go, and that I have no one to follow but the Shepherd. I know the Shepherd will not let me fall over the precipice. He will not let me drink in the swift water, for I might slip and fall in. And I know that no matter what happens, He will go with me, even through "the Valley of the Shadows." With that knowledge, what is there to fear?

He will bring you safely through, no matter which "side of life or death" is your destination. You cannot lose, for He brings His children safely through everything!

Just read this treasured psalm [Psalm 23] every day, and you will be surprised how calm and wonderful you feel.

Helen Steiner Rice

NEW DAY

Lord of the sun which I feel pouring in upon me at the beginning of this new day . . . Lord of the tree that I see swaying just beyond the window of this house . . . Lord of this house in which I live, and of all the years I have spent in it . . . Lord of the days I am yet to spend here, and of the next house to which I move . . . Lord of the eventual home you have prepared for me . . .

Bless this day I am about to begin.

Bless the work I will do in this place so that it will be productive for me and for others. Guide me so that I will use my time wisely. Direct me so that my energies will be spent most effectively.

Time is so precious; don't let me fritter it away on futile, silly things. Yet don't let me drive myself so hard that I don't enjoy it.

Whatever I do, whether large and seemingly important, or something so small as a phone call or making coffee, let it be vital, joyful, blessed with your presence. Enriched with your assurance that it is meaningful. That, however trivial, it really counts in the total scheme of a life composed of hours and days.

Thank you, God, for the marvel and the challenge of this new day.

Marjorie Holmes

Pray and hurl your life after your prayers.

Harry Emerson Fosdick

A PRAYER FOR EVERY DAY

Make me too brave to lie or be unkind.
Make me too understanding, too, to mind
The little hurts companions give, and friends,
The careless hurts that no one quite intends.
Make me too thoughtful to hurt others so.
Help me to know
The inmost hearts of those for whom I care,
Their secret wishes, all the loads they bear,
That I may add my courage to their own.
May I make lonely folks feel less alone,
And happy ones a little happier yet.
May I forget
What ought to be forgotten; and recall
Unfailing, all
That ought to be recalled, each kindly thing,
Forgetting what might sting.
To all upon my way,
Day after day,
Let me be joy, be hope! Let my life sing!

Mary Carolyn Davies

For the Lord thy God bringeth thee into a good land,
a land of brooks of water, of fountains and depths that
spring out of valleys and hills;

A land of wheat, and barley, and vines, and fig trees,
and pomegranates; a land of oil olive, and honey;

25

A land wherein thou shalt eat bread without scarceness, thou shalt not lack any thing in it; a land whose stones are iron, and out of whose hills thou mayest dig brass.

When thou hast eaten and art full, then thou shalt bless the Lord thy God for the good land which he hath given thee.

Deuteronomy 8:7–10

BALANCING

Sometimes
I feel
as if I'm walking a tightrope
and for a balance pole
I need control

control over my temper
control over my impulses
control over my emotions.

Help me keep my balance, Lord,
give me the patience, the power, the perspective
to gain more control
so that I can get from here to there
without falling.

Alice Joyce Davidson

A PARENT'S PRAYER

Oh, God, make me a better parent. Help me to understand my children, to listen patiently to what they have to say and to understand all their questions kindly. Keep me from interrupting them, talking back to them, and contradicting them. Make me as courteous to them as I would have them be to me. Give me the courage to confess my sins against my children and ask them forgiveness, when I know that I have done wrong.

May I not vainly hurt the feelings of my children. Forbid that I should laugh at their mistakes, or resort to shame and ridicule as punishment. Let me not tempt a child to lie and steal. So guide me hour by hour that I may demonstrate by all I say and do that honesty produces happiness.

Reduce, I pray, the meanness in me . . . help me, O Lord, to hold my tongue. Blind me to the little errors of my children as those of their own age. . . . Allow me not to rob them of the opportunity to wait upon themselves, to think, to choose, and to make their own decisions.

Forbid that I should ever punish them for my selfish satisfaction. May I grant them all their wishes that are reasonable and have the courage always to withhold a privilege which I know will do them harm.

Make me so fair and just, so considerate and compassionate to my children that they will have genuine esteem for me. Fit me to be loved and imitated by my children. Oh, God, do give me calm and poise and self-control.

Abigail Van Buren

THE NEW YEAR

Dear Master, for this coming year,
　　Just one request I bring.
I do not pray for happiness
　　Or any earthly thing;
I do not ask to understand
　　The way Thou leadest me;
But this I ask—Teach me to do
　　The thing that pleaseth Thee.
I want to know Thy guiding Voice,
　　To walk with Thee each day.
Dear Master, make me swift to hear
　　And ready to obey;
And thus the year I now begin
　　A happy year will be,
If I am seeking just to do
　　The thing that pleaseth Thee.

Author unknown

III. Humility

"... when ... the soul is on its knees ..."

Victor Hugo

I am a very simple, uncomplicated person, and "a child's faith" is all I possess. There is nothing I need to know, or even try to understand, if I place myself completely in God's great and mighty Hand!

Helen Steiner Rice

From "WHAT IS PRAYER?"

Prayer is the soul's sincere desire,
  Uttered or unexpressed;
The motion of a hidden fire,
  That trembles in the breast.

Prayer is the burden of a sigh,
  The falling of a tear;
The upward glancing of an eye,
  When none but God is near.

James Montgomery

Heaven's gates are not so highly arched as princes' palaces; they that enter there must go upon their knees.

Daniel Webster

We think we must climb to a certain height of goodness before we can reach God. But He says not "At the end of the way you may find me"; He says "I am the Way; I am the road under your feet, the road that begins just as low down as you happen to be." If we are in a hole the Way begins in the hole. The moment we set our face in the same direction as His, we are walking with God.

Helen Wodehouse

Between the humble and the contrite heart and the majesty of heaven there are no barriers; the only password is prayer.

Hosea Ballou

Lord, when we are wrong, make us willing to change. And when we are right, make us easy to live with.

Peter Marshall

MAN ON HIS KNEES

In the early days of the Republic, a stranger once asked Congress how he could distinguish Washington.

He was told, "You can easily distinguish him when Congress goes to prayer. Washington is the gentleman who kneels."

Anonymous

Spend time on your knees and you'll have no trouble standing on your feet.

Perry Tanksley

From "WHAT IS PRAYER?"

O Thou by whom we come to God—
The Life, the Truth, the Way!
The path of prayer Thyself hast trod;
Lord, teach us how to pray!

James Montgomery

HUMILITY

I asked God for strength,
   that I might achieve—
I was made weak,
   that I might learn humbly to obey.

I asked for help
   that I might do greater things—
I was given infirmity,
   that I might do better things.

I asked for riches,
   that I might be happy—
I was given poverty,
   that I might be wise.

I asked for all things,
   that I might enjoy life—
I was given life,
   that I might enjoy all things.

I got nothing
   that I asked for—
But everything
   I had hoped for.

Despite myself,
   my prayers were answered.
I am, among all men,
   most richly blessed.

An anonymous soldier of the Confederacy

I do believe in miracles. I do believe in prayer. I believe completely and without reservation in God. I believe I am a small, struggling sinner, but this does not trouble me too much. I know that if I ask God to forgive me, He will; and I know that He died for me, so who am I to ask Him to explain how His plan will work?

Helen Steiner Rice

Half a proper gardener's work is
done upon his knees.

Rudyard Kipling

Let never day nor night unhallow'd pass,
But still remember what the Lord hath done.

William Shakespeare

Grant us grace, Almighty Father, so to pray as to deserve to be heard.

Jane Austen

Certain thoughts are prayers. There are moments when, whatever be the attitude of the body, the soul is on its knees.

Victor Hugo

O Lord, change the world. Begin, I pray thee, with me.

A Chinese student

May God give us grateful hearts
And keep us mindful
Of the need of others.

Anonymous

IV. Source

of Strength

". . . it will lead you safely . . ."
James Allen

You may be facing some dark hours right now and the clouds of despair at times seem to threaten to close out the light that shines so brightly from your eternal soul. But don't let this happen, for you must remember that dark hours come into the lives of us all. . . .

There are many times when I am ready to give up—but I know that all I have to do is go to God in prayer!

Helen Steiner Rice

Where faith is there is courage, there is fortitude, there is steadfastness and strength . . .

Faith bestows that sublime courage that rises superior to the troubles and disappointments of life, that acknowledges no defeat except as a step to victory; that is strong to endure, patient to wait, and energetic to struggle. . . . Light up, then, the lamp of faith in your heart. . . . It will lead you safely through the mists of doubt and the black darkness of despair; along the narrow, thorny ways of sickness and sorrow, and over the treacherous places of temptation and uncertainty.

James Allen

Prayer begins where human capacity ends.

Norman Vincent Peale

If anyone's presence would have been sufficient to meet the needs of another human being, it would have been the presence of Jesus Christ! And yet, *he prayed* for Peter! Evidently our Lord brought something more to bear on the situation of Peter's weakness and temptable nature than his own presence.

I am not putting down the need for sensitive, affirming, challenging human presence. . . . It is crucial; it is right; but it is not sufficient. When we pray for another, we release the grace of God to a loved one in a way that is not possible in any other method of resourcing. In intercessory prayer, God is able to turn loose powers and strengths that are not otherwise available.

Louis H. Evans, Jr.

Prayer is the most important thing in my life. If I should neglect prayer for a single day, I should lose a great deal of the fire of faith.

Martin Luther

ENGLISH AIR-RAID SHELTER PRAYER

Increase, O God, the spirit of neighborliness among us, that in peril we may uphold one another, in calamity serve one another, in suffering tend one another and in homelessness and loneliness in exile befriend one another. Grant us brave and enduring hearts that we may strengthen one another, till the disciplines and testing of these days be ended, and Thou dost give again peace in our time, through Jesus Christ, our Lord. Amen.

Anonymous

We cannot escape the dangers which abound in life without the actual and *continual* help of God. Let us, then, pray to Him for it continually.

Brother Lawrence

Give us strength to encounter that which is to come, that we may be brave in peril, constant in tribulation, temperate in wrath and in all changes of fortune, and down to the gates of death loyal and loving to one another.

Robert Louis Stevenson

A BUSY MOTHER'S PRAYER

Dear Lord—

You know it isn't that I don't have enough love to go around. It's just that there are so many of them, and my time and strength won't stretch that far.

Today, for instance, I was so busy coaching Bill on English that I couldn't go along with Jeanie to dancing school. She's having trouble with that new song for the recital, too; she wanted me to watch.

But if Bill doesn't pass this special English course he won't get into college. And you know how important that is, especially after losing that time in the service. Yet Jeanie looked so pathetic going off alone with her little suitcase that I felt guilty . . .

And their dad. So often I forget to do the little things he asks me to. I didn't save those clippings. I let the kids get into his tackle box. I'm sometimes so preoccupied in the morning I'm not even sure whether or not I've kissed him good-by. This isn't right. A man needs a good send-off to face the day quite as much as the youngsters do . . .

Choices—all these choices! Between being a den mother for Tommy or a Girl Scout leader for Ruth. Between all the conflicts of music lessons and dental appointments and birthday parties and homework and just plain talking with them seven days a week, sometimes far into the night. No woman can possibly keep up with it all, no matter how hard she tries. Somebody's bound to feel neglected, to think, even if he never says so, "You don't love me as much—"

But you know it isn't any lack of love. It's only lack of energy, of strength, of time. So give me a little extra, please, if possible. And while you're at it, patience, so that I don't get cross and make the problem worse.

Amen.

(And oh, yes, if you could possibly work in an hour or two of peace and quiet and rest for me I'd be so grateful. In fact, it would help all of us a lot!)

Marjorie Holmes

Good Father, I believe that in Christ You will heal all my weaknesses, and they are many and great; but Your medicine is even greater.

St. Augustine

When we get to the place where there's nothing left but God, we find that God is enough.

Author unknown

"JESUS, IT'S JIM . . ."
"JIM, IT'S JESUS"

The preacher, a puzzled frown on his face, hurried to the cottage where the church caretaker lived.

"I am worried," he explained. "Every day at 12 o'clock a shabby old man goes into the church. I can see him through the parsonage window. He only stays a few minutes. It seems most mysterious and you know the altar furnishings are quite valuable. I wish you would keep an eye open, and question the fellow."

The next day, and so for many days, the caretaker watched, and sure enough, at 12 o'clock the shabby figure would arrive.

One day the caretaker accosted him: "Look here, my friend, what are you up to, going into the church every day?"

"I go to pray," the old man replied quietly.

"Now come," the caretaker said sternly, "you don't stay long enough to pray. You are only there a few minutes, for I have watched you. You just go up to the altar every day and then come away."

"Yes, that's true. I cannot pray a long prayer, but every day at 12 o'clock I just come and say, 'Jesus, it's Jim.' Then I wait a minute, then come away. It's just a little prayer, but I guess He hears me."

Some time later poor old Jim was knocked down by a truck, and was taken to the city hospital where he settled down quite happily while his broken leg mended.

The ward where Jim lay had been a sore spot to the hospital nurses for a long time. Some of the men were cross and miserable, others did nothing but grumble from morning till night. Try as the nurses would, the men did not improve.

Then slowly but surely things changed. The men stopped grumbling and were cheerful and contented. They took their medicine, ate their food and settled down without a complaint.

One day, hearing a burst of happy laughter the nurse asked: "What has happened to you all! You are such a nice cheerful lot of patients now. Where have all the grumbles gone?" "Oh, it's old Jim," one patient replied. "He is always so happy, never complains although we know he must be in a lot of pain. He makes us ashamed to make a murmur. No, we can't complain when Jim's around, he's always so cheerful."

The nurse crossed over to where Jim lay. His silvery hair gave him an angelic look. His quiet eyes were full of peace. "Well, Jim," she greeted him, "the men say you are responsible for the change in this ward. They say you are always happy."

"Aye, Nurse, that I am. I can't help being happy. You see, Nurse, it's my visitor. Every day he makes me happy."

"Your visitor?" The nurse was puzzled. She had always noticed that Jim's chair was empty on visiting days, for he was a lonely old man without any relatives. "Your visitor," she repeated. "But when does he come?"

"Every day," Jim replied, the light in his eyes growing brighter. "Yes, every day at 12 o'clock. He comes and stands at the foot of my bed. I see Him, and He smiles and says, 'Jim, it's Jesus.' "

Author unknown

I'm not sure how, but I do know that when people pray to God, they can also communicate their needs to each other. Through prayer we can ask not only for God's resources but for the resources of other persons who may not have any other way of knowing we are in need. When you think about it, that isn't so strange, for if God can communicate with each of us—and I believe he can—certainly he can communicate our needs to each other, thereby releasing whatever resources will benefit us.

Louis H. Evans, Jr.

Almighty God, whose light is of Eternity and knoweth no setting, shine forth and be our safeguard through the night; and though the earth be wrapped in darkness and the heavens be veiled from our sight, let Thy brightness be about our beds, and Thy peace within our souls, and Thy Fatherly blessing upon our sleep this night. Amen.

Author unknown

V. Inner Peace

"... Casting the whole of your care ..."
I Peter 5:7

Dear Lord, grant me Your peace. I do not ask for earthly peace which removes trouble or dulls the senses, but for that holy calm which never fails by day or by night, in joy or in sorrow, but ever lifts the soul to rest upon You. You were so peaceful Yourself, dear Christ, in Your life! Haste and worry and anxiety were never Yours, but a blessed calm which told of mastery. May it not be mine also? Speak to me, Lord. Bid the waves, which seem sometimes so big and threatening, to show themselves as under Your loving control. Touch my wearied heart, that it sink not in despair. Make me glad and brave and joyous always in the knowledge that I am Yours. And in all my ways lead me by Your own hand, and keep me in perfect peace. Amen.

Floyd W. Tomkins

Never wait for fitter time or place to talk to Him. To wait till thou go to church or to thy closet is to make Him wait. He will listen as thou walkest.

George Macdonald

49

GOD BE WITH YOU

May His Counsels Sweet uphold you,
  And His Loving Arms enfold you,
    As you journey on your way.

May His Sheltering Wings protect you,
  And His Light Divine direct you,
    Turning darkness into day.

May His Potent Peace surround you,
  And His Presence linger with you,
    As your inner, golden ray.

Author unknown

A WHIFF OF LILACS

I just had a whiff
a great, big wonderful whiff
of lilacs blooming everywhere . . .
and just like bubbles
my troubles
vanished
in thin
air.

Thank You, God,
for the joy of Your fragrant flowers!

Alice Joyce Davidson

One watches people starting out in life quite adequately, handling life with active vigor, as they run, one after another, into experiences where something deeper than vigor is needed. Serious failure, for example. Some night in his lifetime everyone comes home to find a new guest there—disappointment. What he had set his heart on has gone. . . . If one is to come through difficult experiences unembittered, unspoiled, still a real person, one needs deep resources. . . . Not alone in such experiences as sorrow and failure does this need arise but in man's search for the indispensable spiritual requirements of a satisfying life—inner peace, for example, some serenity in the soul to come home to at night and go out from in the morning. Who does not need that? But no one can get inner peace by pouncing on it, by vigorously willing to have it. Peace is a margin of power around our daily need. Peace is a consciousness of springs too deep for earthly droughts to dry up. Peace is an awareness of reserves from beyond ourselves, so that our power is not so much in us as through us.

Harry Emerson Fosdick

A GRACE

Reveal Thy Presence now, O Lord,
  As in the Upper Room of old;
Break Thou our bread, grace Thou our board,
  And keep our hearts from growing cold.

Thomas Tiplady

51

Truly my soul waiteth upon God.

Psalm 62:1

O Lord our God, even at this moment as we come blundering into Thy presence in prayer, we are haunted by memories of duties unperformed, promptings disobeyed, and beckonings ignored.

Opportunities to be kind knocked on the door of our hearts and went weeping away.

We are ashamed, O Lord, and tired of failure.

If Thou art drawing close to us now, come nearer still, till selfishness is burned out within us and our wills lose their weakness in union with Thine own. Amen.

Peter Marshall

Christ be with me, Christ within me,
Christ behind me, Christ before me,
Christ beside me, Christ to win me,
Christ to comfort and restore me,
Christ beneath me, Christ above me,
Christ in quiet, Christ in danger,
Christ in hearts of all that love me,
Christ in mouth of friend and stranger.

St. Patrick

LONESOME

Dear Master, I am lonesome;
  Dear Master, speak to me!
I've been longing here at twilight
  For the voices o'er the sea,
And it seems as if my heartache
  Would be hushed, less piercing be,
If Thou, Lord, wouldst come still closer—
  I am lonesome; speak to me!

I've been thinking in the stillness,
  As I've watched the sunset glow
Die out yonder on the hilltop,
  Leaving naught but cold and woe—
I've been thinking of the faces
  That have come a-trooping by,
Old-time faces, long-time vanished.
  Leaving me to wait and sigh;

And I'm lonesome, Lord, I'm lonesome;
  Come Thou closer; speak to me,
For I'm listening here at twilight
  To the voices o'er the sea,
And it seems as if my heartache
  Would be hushed, less piercing be,
If Thou, Lord, wouldst come still closer—
  I am lonesome; speak to me!

Ralph Spaulding Cushman

ON THE WINGS OF PRAYER

Just close your eyes and open your heart
And feel your worries and cares depart,
Just yield yourself to the Father above
And let Him hold you secure in His love . . .
For life on earth grows more involved
With endless problems that can't be solved—
But God only asks us to do our best,
Then He will "take over" and finish the rest . . .
So when you are tired, discouraged and blue,
There's always one door that is open to you—
And that is the door to *The House of Prayer*
And you'll find God waiting to meet you there . . .
And *The House of Prayer* is no farther away
Than the quiet spot where you kneel and pray—
For the heart is a temple when God is there
As we place ourselves in His loving care.
And He hears every prayer and answers each one
When we pray in His name *Thy will be done*—
And the burdens that seemed too heavy to bear
Are lifted away on *the wings of prayer.*

Helen Steiner Rice

O make in me those civil wars to
cease!

Sir Philip Sidney

In a world where
> there is so much to ruffle the spirit, how needful that entering into the secret of God's pavilion, which will alone bring it back to composure and peace!

In a world where
> there is so much to sadden and depress, how blessed the communion with Him in whom is the one true source and fountain of all true gladness and abiding joy!

In a world where
> so much is ever seeking to unhallow our spirits, to render them common and profane, how high the privilege of consecrating them anew in prayer to holiness and to God.

Archbishop Richard Chenevix Trench

IT'S NEVER EASY

It's never easy when one must go
    And one must stay—behind;
It's never easy, I know, I know—
    It sears both heart and mind.

It's never easy, but go one must
    When comes the day, the hour;
It's never easy, but if we trust,
    God will give strength and power.

It's never easy! God knows this, too;
   That's why He stays quite near
To help us as we stumble through
   The vale of grief and fear.

It's never easy, but take God's hand
   And pray till night has passed;
Just trust nor ask to understand—
   And peace will come—at last.

Phyllis C. Michael

The sovereign cure for worry is
prayer.

William James

NO FAVOR DO I SEEK TODAY

I come not to ASK, to PLEAD or IMPLORE You,
I just come to tell You HOW MUCH I ADORE You.
For to kneel in Your Presence makes me feel blest
For I know that You know all my needs best . . .
And it fills me with joy just to linger with You
As my soul You replenish and my heart You renew,
For prayer is much more than just asking for things—
It's the PEACE and CONTENTMENT that QUIET-
   NESS brings . . .
So thank You again for Your MERCY and LOVE
And for making me heir to YOUR KINGDOM
   ABOVE!

Helen Steiner Rice

Immediately you awake set your first thought on God. Keep your mind on him for a few seconds. Do not think of him subjectively, as to your relation to him, your failures, your sins, or your needs, but rather objectively. Let your whole self become conscious of him. Think of him as shining beauty, radiant joy, creative power, all-pervading love, perfect understanding, purity, and serenity. This need only take a moment or two once the habit has been formed, but it is of inestimable importance. It sets the tone for the whole day. . . .

One's waking mood tends to correspond to the state of mind in which one falls asleep. If, therefore, as a result of a disturbed night or simply because of lack of practice, this first thought of God should evade you, look out of the window for something obviously made by him, trees, flowers, the sky, or a wind-shaped cloud, even a gray one, and ponder on the perfection of his handicraft. . . .

Never get into bed with a burdened or a heavy mind; whether it be a vague oppression or a definite fear, shame or remorse, anger or hate, get rid of the evil thing before you lie down to sleep. Night is a holy time, a time of renewing and refreshment. He giveth to his beloved while they sleep; our unconscious mind is active during our slumber. Settle down restfully to let your mind get clear and your spirit unclogged.

Muriel Lester

If the heart wanders or is distracted, bring it back to the point quite gently and replace it tenderly in its Master's presence. And even if you did nothing during the whole of your hour but bring your heart back and place it again in Our Lord's presence, though it went away every time you brought it back, your hour would be very well employed.

St. Francis de Sales

I pray thee, O God, that I may be beautiful within.

Socrates

EVENSONG

The embers of the day are red
Beyond the murky hill.
The kitchen smokes; the bed
In the darkling house is spread:
The great sky darkens overhead,
And the great woods are shrill.
So far have I been led,
Lord, by Thy will:
So far I have followed, Lord, and wondered still.
The breeze from the embalmed land
Blows sudden towards the shore,
And claps my cottage door.
I hear the signal, Lord—I understand.
The night at Thy command
Comes. I will eat and sleep and will not question more.

Robert Louis Stevenson

Casting the whole of your care—
all your anxieties, all your worries,
all your concerns, once and for
all—on Him; for He cares for you
affectionately, and cares about you
watchfully.

I Peter 5:7, Amplified Bible

VI. Answered Prayer

"... But this I know:

      God answers prayer ..."
              Eliza M. Hickok

Ask, and it shall be given you;
seek, and ye shall find; knock, and
it shall be opened unto you.

Matthew 7:7

God is bound to act, to pour
Himself into thee as soon as He
shall find thee ready.

Meister Johannes Eckhart

When in prayer you clasp your hands,
God opens His.

German proverb

ONE DAY AT A TIME

One day at a time, with its failures and fears,
With its hurts and mistakes, with its weakness and tears,
With its portion of pain and its burden of care;
One day at a time we must meet and must bear.
One day at a time—but the day is so long.
And the heart is not brave, and the soul is not strong.
O Thou pitiful Christ, be Thou near all the way:
Give courage and patience and strength for the day.

Swift cometh His answer, so clear and so sweet;
"Yea, I will be with thee, thy troubles to meet;
I will not forget thee, nor fail thee, nor grieve;
I will not forsake thee; I will never leave."
One day at a time, and the day is His day;
He hath numbered its hours, though they haste or
    delay,
His grace is sufficient; we walk not alone;
As the day, so the strength that He giveth His own.

Annie Johnson Flint

When it is hardest to pray, we
must pray the hardest.

Perry Tanksley

64

GOD'S WILL

I know not by what methods rare,
But this I know: God answers prayer.
I know not if the blessing sought
Will come in just the guise I thought.
I leave my prayer to Him alone
Whose will is wiser than my own.

Eliza M. Hickok

Jesus spoke about how prayer can remove mountains. However, we need to remember there are two ways by which a mountain can cease to block our paths. One way is to move it. The other is to develop the strength to walk over the top of the mountain and keep going. In answer to our prayers, sometimes God takes away our handicaps; at other times He gives us the strength to keep going in spite of what has happened.

Charles L. Allen

When we bless God for mercies, we prolong them.
When we bless God for miseries, we usually end them.

Charles Haddon Spurgeon

ON HIS OWN TWO FEET

The boy had fallen, running home after school, and skinned his left knee. It was no more than a scratch—there wasn't even a rent in his trousers—but by night the knee started to ache. Nothing much, he thought, being 13 and the sturdy son of a frontiersman. Ignoring the pain, he knelt in his nightgown and said his prayers, then climbed into bed in the room where he and his five brothers slept.

His leg was painful the next morning, but he still did not tell anyone. The farm kept the whole family relentlessly busy; always he had to be up at six to do his chores before school. And he must be thorough about them or he would be sent back to do them over again, no matter what else he had to miss, including meals. In their household, discipline was fair but stern.

Two mornings later the leg ached too badly for him to drag himself to the barn. That was a Sunday and he could remain behind, while the rest of the family drove into town. School homework finished, he sat in the parlor rocker, examining and comparing the three family Bibles: one in German that held the records of all their births and deaths; another in Greek that was his father's proud possession; and finally the King James version shared by mother and all the sons.

One night this week it would be the boy's turn to lead the family devotions. He could select his own passages from the Old and New Testaments and read them aloud and try to get a discussion going; sometimes they became exciting. But now the pain blurred his attention;

he put aside the Scriptures and dozed until his brothers returned from Sunday School.

By the time dinner was ready the boy had climbed into bed. The shoe had to be cut off his swollen and discolored leg. Why on earth hadn't he told somebody? Go quick and fetch the doctor!

Mother bathed knee and foot and thigh, applied poultices and wiped the boy's sweating forehead with a moist, cool cloth. She was an intense and vital woman. Confronted with this angry infection, her manner remained serene. Mom had nursed her brood through accidents and ailments from toothaches to scarlet fever; one son she had lost, but that only made her calmer and more determined when she had to fight for the others.

Old Dr. Conklin examined the leg and pursed his lips. "It's not likely we can save it!"

The invalid sat up stiffly. "What's that mean?" he asked huskily.

"It means," explained the doctor gently, "if things get worse we'll have to amputate."

"Not me!" stormed the boy. "I won't have it! I'd rather die!"

"The longer we wait, the more we have to take off," urged the doctor.

"You won't take any off!" The boy's voice broke with an adolescent crack, as his mother turned away, shaken. But there was no adolescence in the eyes that defied the doctor's reproachful gaze.

Dr. Conklin stalked out, nodding to the mother to follow him. As he stood in the hallway explaining to both parents about what could and probably would happen, they could hear the boy calling for his brother: "Ed! *Ed*! Come up here, will you?"

The brother stamped in and then they heard the sick lad's voice, high pitched with pain: "If I go out of my head, Ed, don't let them cut off my leg. Promise me, Ed—*promise*!"

In a moment Ed came out and stood outside the bedroom door, his arms folded. Quite clearly he was standing on guard.

Ed looked straight at old Dr. Conklin. "Nobody's going to saw off that leg!" he announced.

"But, Ed—you'll be sorry," gasped the doctor.

"Maybe so, Doc. But I gave him my word."

And nothing changed that.

If Ed had not stood his ground, father and mother might have yielded. They were not yet convinced that amputation was necessary; they were doubtful. The adamant attitude first of the sick boy and then of his brother was incredible, for defiance of parental authority was unknown in this household. Yet there was Ed, standing before the sickroom door.

"Guess we'll wait and see how he looks by tonight, eh, Doc?" said the father.

For two days and nights Ed stood guard, sleeping at the threshold, not leaving even to eat. The fever mounted, and the suffering boy babbled in torment, but the older brother showed no weakening of resolve, even though the discoloration of the swollen leg was creeping toward the pelvis, just as the doctor had predicted. Ed remained firm because he had given his promise, and also because he shared the frontiersmen's horror of being less than physically perfect.

The parents knew that their son would never forgive an amputation, and Ed's attitude continued to be decisive, time after time, when the doctor returned. Once, in helpless rage, Dr. Conklin shouted, "It's murder!" and slammed the front door. Nothing but a miracle could save the boy now!

Mother, father and watchful brother Ed shared the same thought, as their anxious eyes turned from the doorway. Had they forgotten their faith in the turmoil of their fears? Now, in this desperate hour, the three went to their knees at the bedside.

They prayed, taking turns in leading one another. Father, mother—and at last Edgar—would rise and go about the farm work and rejoin the continual prayer. During the second night the other four brothers would kneel from time to time and join in the prayers.

The next morning, when the faithful old doctor stopped by again, his experienced eye saw a sign. The swelling was going down! Dr. Conklin closed his eyes and made a rusty prayer of his own—a prayer of thanksgiving. Even after the boy dropped into a normal sleep, one member of the family after another kept the prayer vigil.

It was nightfall again and the lamps were lighted when the boy opened his eyes. The swelling was away down now, and the discoloration had almost faded. In three weeks—pale and weak, but with eyes clear and voice strong—the boy could stand up.

And Ike Eisenhower was ready to face life.

Grace Perkins Oursler

All things, whatsoever ye shall ask in prayer, believing, ye shall receive.

Matthew 21:22

ALL PRAYER IS ANSWERED

Why doubt that God answers prayer?
To most of us who pray,
He replies with a simple "No,"
Or else says, "Not today."
We complain, "But that's no answer,"
Because we're unaware
God's No or Wait is often
A perfect answer to prayer.
At other times we're burdened down
So much we pray and fast,
And God replies, "Go work it out;
You bring it to pass."
Let us give thanks for positive answers
But think it not unusual
That God's best answer often is
Postponement and refusal.

Perry Tanksley

VII. Adoration and Praise

"... I yield Thee praise ..."

Philip Jerome Cleveland

We are not the same as we were when we began to pray. We have touched God, and we have opened our lives to him—not only for the moments it took us to pray, but for all time. How can we help but rise up in confidence, blessing God for his magnificence, his power, his glory, and—wonder of wonders!—his love for us!

Colleen Townsend Evans

LET US WITH
A GLADSOME MIND

Let us with a gladsome mind
Praise the Lord, for he is kind;
For his mercies aye endure,
Ever faithful, ever sure.
John Milton

Thanks be unto God for his unspeakable gift.

II Corinthians 9:15

I YIELD THEE PRAISE

For thoughts that curve like winging birds
Out of the summer dusk each time
I drink the splendor of the sky
And touch the wood-winds swinging by—
I yield Thee praise.

For waves that lift from autumn seas
To spill strange music on the land,
The broken nocturne of a lark
Flung out upon the lonely dark—
I yield Thee praise.

For rain that piles gray torrents down
Black mountain-gullies to the plain,
For singing fields and crimson flare
At daybreak, and the sea-sweet air—
I yield Thee praise.

For gentle mists that wander in
To hide the tired world outside
That in our hearts old lips may smile
Their blessing through life's afterwhile—
I yield Thee praise.

For hopes that fight like stubborn grass
Up through the clinging snows of fear
To find the rich earth richer still
With kindliness and honest will—
I yield Thee praise.

Philip Jerome Cleveland

I cannot conceive how a man could look up into the heavens and say there is no God.

Abraham Lincoln

A grateful thought toward heaven is of itself a prayer.

Gotthold Ephraim Lessing

SUDDEN PRAYER

Now, Lord, I turn to Thee,
Having no other need
For now, except to be
With Thee, my spirit freed
Of askings and desires
With nothing to implore.
One thing my soul requires,
To worship, to adore.

Jane Merchant

NO WORD HAS FAILED

Lord, help us to thank Thee as we should
For this, Thy constant care:
For the good wheat for our daily bread,
For the outdoor pure clean air,
For the fruits of garden, field and tree
That tell anew Thy constancy;
Back of all these we see Thy hand
Opened to every need;
We see Thy might and mercy, Lord,
In each small jewelled seed;
May we walk with singing hearts of praise
Through all Thy glowing, golden days.

Grace Noll Crowell

Our heavenly Father,
we adore Thee,
whose name is love,
whose nature is compassion,
whose presence is joy,
whose word is truth,
whose spirit is goodness,
whose holiness is beauty,
whose will is peace,
whose service is perfect freedom,
and in knowledge of whom
        standeth our eternal life.

Author unknown

SING GOD'S PRAISES

When I look at God's flowers
Or feel His cool breeze,
Or taste the sweet gifts
From His fruit-bearing trees . . .
      My heart sings!

When I study the stars
That light up the sky,
Or watch a young fledgling
Just learning to fly . . .
      My heart sings!

When I marvel at nature,
Each miracle of
God's awesome creation
He fashioned with love . . .
      My heart sings!

And, when my heart's singing,
I offer a prayer
Of thanks for His bountiful gifts
Which I share,
And as I am praying,
I feel His great care . . .
      And my heart sings!

Alice Joyce Davidson

Gratitude is the song of the soul in the presence of the goodness of God.

W. T. Purkiser

From "THE COMMON QUESTION"

The dear God hears and pities all;
    He knoweth all our wants;
And what we blindly ask of Him
    His love withholds or grants.

And so I sometimes think our prayers
    Might well be merged in one;
And nest and perch and hearth and church
    Repeat, "Thy will be done."

John Greenleaf Whittier

A HEART TO PRAISE THEE

Thou hast given so much to me,
Give one thing more—a grateful heart:
Not thankful when it pleaseth me,
As if thy blessings had spare days,
But such a heart whose Pulse may be
Thy Praise.

George Herbert

From "A SUN-DAY HYMN"

Lord of all life, below, above,
Whose light is truth, whose warmth is love,
Before thy ever-blazing throne
We ask no lustre of our own.

Grant us thy truth to make us free,
And kindling hearts that burn for thee,
Till all thy living altars claim
One holy light, one heavenly flame!

Oliver Wendell Holmes

Praise ye the Lord.
Praise God in his sanctuary:
    praise him in the firmament of his power.
Praise him for his mighty acts:
    praise him according to his excellent greatness.
Praise him with the sound of the trumpet:
    praise him with the psaltery and harp.
Praise him with the timbrel and dance:
    praise him with stringed instruments and organs.
Praise him upon the loud cymbals:
    praise him upon the high sounding cymbals.
Let every thing that hath breath praise the Lord.
Praise ye the Lord.

Psalm 150

THANK YOU, GOD, FOR EVERYTHING

Thank you, God, for everything—
  the big things and the small,
For "every good gift comes from God"—
  the giver of them all—
And all too often we accept
  without any thanks or praise
The gifts God sends as blessings
  each day in many ways,
And so at this THANKSGIVING TIME
  we offer up a prayer
To thank you, God, for giving us
  a lot more than our share . . .
First, thank you for the little things
  that often come our way,
The things we take for granted
  but don't mention when we pray,

The unexpected courtesy,
   the thoughtful, kindly deed,
A hand reached out to help us
   in the time of sudden need . . .
Oh, make us more aware, dear God,
   of little daily graces
That come to us with "sweet surprise"
   from never-dreamed-of places—
Then, thank you for the "MIRACLES"
   we are much too blind to see,
And give us new awareness
   of our many gifts from Thee,
And help us to remember
   that the KEY to LIFE and LIVING
Is to make each prayer a PRAYER of THANKS
   and every day THANKSGIVING.

Helen Steiner Rice

VIII. *Every Day*

"... let me sow love ..."
                    St. Francis of Assisi

O Lord, Thou knowest how
busy I must be this day. If I forget
Thee, do not forget me.

Sir Jacob Ashley

FOR THE MORNING

You are ushering in another day
Untouched and freshly new,
So here I come to ask You, God,
If you'll renew me, too.
Forgive the many errors
That I made yesterday
And let me try again, dear God,
To walk closer in Thy way. . . .
But, Father, I am well aware
I can't make it on my own.
So take my hand and hold it tight
For I can't walk alone.

Helen Steiner Rice

I thank Thee for the house in which I live,
    For the gray roof on which the raindrops slant;
I thank Thee for a garden and the slim young shoots
    That mark old-fashioned things I plant.

I thank Thee for a daily task to do,
    For books that are my ships with golden wings,
For mighty gifts let others offer praise—
    Lord, I am thanking Thee for little things.

Author unknown

If a child lives with criticism, he learns to condemn.
If a child lives with hostility, he learns to fight.
If a child lives with ridicule, he learns to be shy.
If a child lives with shame, he learns to feel guilty.
If a child lives with tolerance, he learns to be patient.
If a child lives with encouragement, he learns confidence.
If a child lives with praise, he learns to appreciate.
If a child lives with fairness, he learns justice.
If a child lives with security, he learns to have faith.
If a child lives with approval, he learns to like himself.
If a child lives with acceptance and friendship,
HE LEARNS TO FIND LOVE IN THE WORLD.
May we learn to give encouragement, praise, fairness, security, approval, acceptance and friendship to our child and other children.

Dorothy Nolte

A PRAYER FOR PARENTS

Build me a son, O Lord, who will be strong enough to know when he is weak, and brave enough to face himself when he is afraid; one who will be proud and unbending in honest defeat, and humble and gentle in victory.

Build me a son whose wishbone will not be where his backbone should be; a son who will know Thee—and that to know himself is the foundation stone of knowledge.

Lead him, I pray, not in the path of ease and comfort, but under the stress and spur of difficulties and challenge. Here, let him learn to stand up in the storm; here, let him learn compassion for those who fail.

Build me a son whose heart will be clear, whose goal will be high; a son who will master himself before he seeks to master other men; one who will learn to laugh, yet never forget how to weep; one who will reach into the future, yet never forget the past.

And after all these things are his, add, I pray, enough of a sense of humor, so that he may always be serious, yet never take himself too seriously. Give him humility, so that he may always remember the simplicity of true greatness, the open mind of true wisdom, the meekness of true strength. Then I, his father, will dare to whisper, "I have not lived in vain."

General Douglas A. MacArthur

Father, I believe that a home not built on the rock of faith hasn't a chance.

Help me to give my children a chance.

Dale Evans Rogers

Lord Jesus, You who bade the children come
And took them in Your gentle arms and smiled,
Grant me unfailing patience through the day
To understand and help my little child.

I would not only give his body care
And guide his young dependent steps along
The wholesome ways, but I would know his heart,
Attuning mine to childhood's griefs and song.

Oh, give me vision to discern the child
Behind whatever he may do or say,
The wise humility to learn from him
The while I strive to teach him day by day.

Adelaide Love

Lord, make me an instrument of your peace.
Where there is hatred, let me sow love;
where there is injury, pardon;
where there is doubt, faith;
where there is despair, hope;
where there is darkness, light;
and where there is sadness, joy.

St. Francis of Assisi

God, give us grace to accept with
serenity the things that cannot be
changed, courage to change the
things which should be changed,
and the wisdom to distinguish the
one from the other.

Reinhold Niebuhr

Today, Lord, our son/daughter goes to school for the
first time. We shouldn't be but we are anxious. It will be
funny without him/her. Yet we will have the joy of being
together once more at the end of the school day. Be with
our beloved, our precious one. May we all learn to live in
your care.

Tony Jasper

A SALESMAN'S PRAYER

Oh creator of all things, help me. For this day I go out into the world naked and alone, and without your hand to guide me I will wander far from the path which leads to success and happiness.

I ask not for gold or garments or even opportunities equal to my ability; instead, guide me so that I may acquire ability equal to my opportunities.

You have taught the lion and the eagle how to hunt and prosper with teeth and claw. Teach me how to hunt with words and prosper with love so that I may be a lion among men and an eagle in the market place.

Help me to remain humble through obstacles and failures; yet hide not from mine eyes the prize that will come with victory.

Assign me tasks to which others have failed; yet guide me to pluck the seeds of success from their failures. Confront me with fears that will temper my spirit; yet endow me with courage to laugh at my misgivings.

Spare me sufficient days to reach my goals; yet help me to live this day as though it be my last.

Guide me in my words that they may bear fruit; yet silence me from gossip that none be maligned.

Discipline me in the habit of trying and trying again; yet show me the way to make use of the law of averages. Favor me with alertness to recognize opportunity; yet endow me with patience which will concentrate my strength.

Bathe me in good habits that the bad ones may drown; yet grant me compassion for weaknesses in others. Suffer me to know that all things shall pass; yet help me to count my blessings of today.

Expose me to hate so it not be a stranger; yet fill my cup with love to turn strangers into friends.

But all these things be only if thy will. I am a small and a lonely grape clutching the vine, yet thou hast made me different from all others. Verily, there must be a special place for me. Guide me. Help me. Show me the way.

Let me become all you planned for me when my seed was planted and selected by you to sprout in the vineyard of the world.

Help this humble salesman. Guide me, God.

Og Mandino

Thank God for dirty dishes;
They have a story to tell.
And by the stack I have
It seems we are living very well.
While people of other countries are starving
I haven't the heart to fuss,
For by this stack of evidence
God's awfully good to us.

A high school girl

LAUGHTER

Thank you for laughter—
it changed my world, today!

I was harassed and all put-about;
my day had gone completely up the creek:
I seemed to be fighting time
single-handed.
Suddenly, floating up from that flat below
and in through my open window
where I was sitting working at my thesis,
came the sound of children
laughing!
A clear, delightful sound.
I looked out
and there they were,
these little girls
playing with a kitten.

It saved the day for me.
Thank you . . .
and the children!

Major Joy Webb, S.A.

Dear Lord, here at the beginning of my life, I want desperately to know two things: who I am, and what you would have me do with my one life. I must know, soon. Could you let me know, Lord?

Author unknown

O God, sometimes I am tempted
because cheating seems to be the easiest
and quickest way to get what I want.
Forgive me for the times
I have told lies, kept miscounted change,
or misled my friends. Grant that I shall come to
love truth and hate lies—especially my own. May all
my words and deeds be free of sham and make-believe.

In the classroom, in games
with my friends, as I trade at the store, help me
to be completely trustworthy.

Day by day may I live
in such close friendship with Thee that there will be
nothing in my life
which is counterfeit or insincere. Amen.

Walter L. Cook

Day by day,
O Lord,
three things I pray:
to see thee more clearly,
love thee more dearly,
follow thee more nearly,
day by day.

St. Richard of Chichester

AN AWFUL DAY

Today, Lord, has been awful!
It started badly,
Imps of depression sat on the bedposts
waiting for me to wake,
ready to pounce on me,
to harry me
and fill me with their gloom.

My head ached, my nerves were edgy
and I felt irritable.

And then it rained . . .
not a decent sort of rain, soon over and done with,
but a penetrating, miserable, drooling kind of rain
that wet-blanketed soul as well as body.

There are days like that, Master.
Days when life is heavy, boring, meaningless;
days when no ray pierces the inward gloom,
just plain bad days.

What is your recipe for such hours, Lord?
I am reminded of some words which were often on your
        lips:
"Take heart!"
They must have comforted your followers many times.
You used them when they were startled,
when they had lost their nerve,
when they needed encouragement.

I need encouragement, Master,
so I quieten my mind and wait to hear you say:
"Take heart!"
Thank you, Lord.

Flora Larsson, S.A.

Help me, O God, to be a good and a true friend:
to be always loyal, and never to let my friends down;
never to talk about them behind their backs in a way in
    which I would not do before their faces;
never to betray a confidence or talk about the things
    about which I ought to be silent;
always to be ready to share everything I have;
to be as true to my friends as I would wish them to be to
    me.

This I ask for the sake of him who is the greatest and the
    truest of all friends, for Jesus' sake. Amen.

William Barclay

There is no use
Giving a snow job to you, Lord.
You already know me like a book.

So when I'm all alone
Help me to see me like I am
Even if I don't like it.

Inside of me I want the right thing,
Then when I'm with someone
I want them to think I'm the big man.

When I'm all alone tonight, God,
Help me see
What you want me to be like.

Carl F. Burke

Give us grace, O Lord, to work
while it is day, fulfilling diligently
and patiently whatever duty Thou
appointest us; doing small things
in the day of small things, and
great labours if Thou summonest
us to any; rising and working, sitting still and suffering according
to Thy word.

Christina Rossetti

The rich young man scares me.

I am scared by the story of the young man who met the
  Christ himself and yet turned his back and walked
  away.

His "riches" were too much for him.
He closed his eyes to the needs of others,
and shut out the Master
who could have given him true greatness.

I am scared because my eyes want to close, too.
The one who turned his back lives very near,
while He seems far away.

Lord of life,
fill my conscience full of thy spirit of love.
Occupy my mind. Subdue my selfishness.

Grant me, dear God,
the strength to face with firmness
my brother and my Master,
that what I am and have will serve thy will.
and all my walking will be on the path
of his divine steps. Amen.

James O. Gilliom

Great Spirit, help me never to
judge another until I have walked
in his moccasins.

Sioux prayer

A WEDDING ANNIVERSARY

Lord, today we thank you for each other. The years go so quickly and yet we know now that we are a part of each other. We thank you for all the laughter we have shared, our private jokes, our funny habits.

We thank you for the times when we have been a strength to each other; for what we might have lacked apart we found together.

We thank you for the day-by-day adventure of being man and wife—for the companionship, help and comfort that we have given to each other.

There's more yet. Help us to grow closer to each other and to you in everything that is yet to be.

Michael Walker

They came for our child, Lord. It had to be, for he/she was in such pain. So now we worry and pace the room. Oh, we do hope the operation will be successful. We do hope so. Thank you for this time in prayer. Be with the doctors, surgeons and nurses who tend our little one. Be with all other parents who this day are like us. It's going to be a long, long evening and night. With you we can cope.

Tony Jasper

Lord of all pots and pans and things, since I've no time
to be
A saint by doing lovely things or watching late with
Thee,
Or dreaming in the dawnlight or storming heaven's
gates,
Make me a saint by getting meals and washing up the
plates.

Although I must have Martha's hands, I have a Mary
mind;
And as I black the boots and shoes, Thy sandals, Lord, I
find.
I think of how they trod the earth; what time I scrub the
floor;
Accept this meditation, Lord; I haven't time for more.

Warm all the kitchen with Thy love, and light it with
Thy peace;
Forgive me all my worryings, and make all grumblings
cease.
Thou who didst love to give men food, in room or by the
sea,
Accept this service that I do—I do it unto Thee.

Cecily Hallack

Lord, help me live from day to day
In such a self-forgetful way,
That even when I kneel to pray,
My prayer may be for—*others*.

Charles Dickens

Lord Jesus, bless all who serve us, who have dedicated their lives to the ministry of others—all the teachers in our schools who labor so patiently with so little appreciation; all who wait upon the public, the clerks in the stores who have to accept criticism, complaints, bad manners, selfishness, at the hands of a thoughtless public. Bless the mailmen, the drivers of streetcars and buses who must listen to people who have lost their tempers.

Bless every humble soul who, in these days of stress and strain, preaches sermons without words.

Peter Marshall

Grant that I may not so much seek to be consoled as to
    console;
to be understood as to understand;
to be loved as to love;
for it is in giving that we receive,
it is in pardoning that we are pardoned.

St. Francis of Assisi

Lord,
why is it so difficult
to make peace with each other?
No wonder there are wars.
Is it pride that holds
my mouth tight:
a childish feeling
that I am not the one
who should apologize?
It wasn't my fault?
In these flare-ups
what does it matter
whose fault it is?
The only thing that matters
is love and harmony.
Lord, turning my back
in anger is weakness,
it reduces me as a human being.
Give me the courage,
the stature
to say, "I'm sorry."

Frank Topping

May the road rise up to meet you,
May the wind be always at your back,
May the sun shine warm upon your face,
And the rain fall soft upon your fields,
And until we meet again,
May God hold you in the palm of His hand.

Gaelic prayer

Index of Authors

Index of Titles

Index of First Lines

God is bound to act, 63
Good Father, I believe that in Christ, 43
Grant that I may not so much seek to be consoled, 100
Grant us grace, Almighty Father, 36
Gratitude is the song of the soul, 78
Great Spirit, help me never to judge, 97

Half a proper gardener's work, 35
Heaven's gates are not so highly arched, 32
Help me, O God, to be a good and a true friend, 95
Help us this day, O God, 21

I am a very simple, uncomplicated person, 31
I asked God for strength, 34
I cannot conceive how a man could look up, 75
I come not to ASK, to PLEAD or IMPLORE You, 56
I do believe in miracles, 35
If a child lives with criticism, he learns to condemn, 86
If anyone's presence would have been sufficient, 40
If the heart wanders, 58
I just had a whiff, 50
I know not by what methods rare, 65
I met God in the morning, 14
Immediately you awake, 57
I'm not sure how, but I do know, 46
In a world where, 55
Increase, O God, the spirit of neighborliness, 41
In the early days of the Republic, 33
I pray thee, O God, that I may be, 58
I thank Thee for the house in which I live, 86
It is only when men begin to worship, 13
It's never easy when one must go, 55
I walk with God daily, 21

Jesus spoke about how prayer can remove mountains, 65
Just close your eyes and open your heart, 54
Just think what it means to know that the Lord, 23

Let never day nor night unhallow'd pass, 35
Let us with a gladsome mind, 73
Lord, help me live from day to day, 99
Lord, help us to thank Thee as we should, 76
Lord Jesus, bless all who serve us, 100
Lord Jesus, You who bade the children come, 88
Lord, make me an instrument of your peace, 89
Lord of all life, below, above, 79
Lord of all pots and pans and things, since I've no time to be, 99
Lord of the sun, 24
Lord, today we thank you for each other, 98
Lord, when we are wrong, 32
Lord, why is it so difficult, 101

Make me too brave to lie or be unkind, 25
May every soul that touches mine, 17
May God give us grateful hearts, 36
May His Counsels Sweet uphold you, 50
May I seek to live this day, 22
May the road rise up to meet you, 102

Never wait for fitter time or place, 49
Now, Lord, I turn to Thee, 75

O God of Easter, God of resurrection power, 15
O God, sometimes I am tempted, 93
Oh creator of all things, help me, 90
Oh, God, make me a better parent, 27
O Lord, change the world, 36
O Lord our God, even at this moment, 52
O Lord, Thou knowest how busy I must be, 85
O make in me those civil wars, 54
One day at a time, with its failures and fears, 64
One watches people starting out in life, 51
O Thou by whom we come to God, 33
Our heavenly Father, 76

When I look at God's flowers, 77
When in prayer you clasp your hands, 63
When it is hardest to pray, 64
When we bless God for mercies, we prolong them, 65
When we get to the place, 43
Where faith is there is courage, 39
Why doubt that God answers prayer, 70

You are ushering in another day, 85
You know it isn't that I don't have enough love, 42
You may be facing some dark hours, 39